Heart Of The Turtle

A Parkinson Patient Asks:
"Why *NOT* Mercury Dr. Lieberman?
Quicksilver

BY

Rebecca K. Hudson

[handwritten inscription: Dear Pat / ...thanks for / your interest / in my / art, / love Becky]

eBookstand Books
www.ebookstand.com

eBOOKSTAND

*Thanks for your help & interest
in my art.
Love. Becky 4-29-05*

Published by
eBookstand Books
Division of CyberRead, Inc.
Houston, TX 77079
1827_10

ISBN 1-58909-189-2

Printed in the United States of America

Forward

Seldom in life does one get the privilege of encountering a human being who survives on courage from moment to moment, and from day to day. Seldom in life does one have the rare opportunity to be introduced to the artistic expression of such a person. Such is the experience you are about to encounter upon opening the pages of this extraordinary book of art and verse. Author and artist, Rebecca Hudson has combined her gift of painting with her gift of prose, drawing the reader into a world that few of us have experienced, a place of those souls who are experiencing a deteriorating chronic illness from day to day. However this is not a book about disease; rather, it is a book about life.

Rebecca Hudson has written this important work within the daily pain and spasms of Parkinson's disease. Chronic illness has a tendency to take a person to the depths of understanding about life's priorities. There no longer remains energy for shallow thought but instead significant contributions of purified enlightenment. Yet, most of society does not get the opportunity to learn from the enlightened chronically ill. Here is such an opportunity.

Marcia Hoover

For my father, Verne Lyle Hudson.

William Fetter, who suggested I assemble a book of my work, and provided its design and direction. Also Barbara Fetter, for her graciousness, patience, and hospitality.

Dennis J. Hughes, PhD., Presbyterian Minister and Jungian Therapist.

Marcia Hoover, M.S., counselor for the chronically ill, who "watched over me" for two years, and encouraged me to publish this book.

Sharon Gayle Rabb for overseeing the assembly and completion of this book, including editing and typing.

John Benjamin Rodgers, who helped with editing, typing and sample text.

Thank you Neil Rogers.

Tess Sterling, who opened her store, Stargazers, to my work.

Thanks to John Moore for sharing the information that saved his life from Mercury poisoning.

Thanks to Mercury Man.

And a special acknowledgment and thanks to those who pray for others who are troubled or get lost in despair, and have no one else to pray for them.

Acknowledgments

Thanks to Marilyn and Fené for always being there
when we needed you.

Contents

To My Readers,

I offer these few pages of text to the Mercury Man's Message, written of simple logic to make key points.

What Would It Mean If Mercury Caused Parkinson's?

becky: When I began work on this book 18 years ago, the foremost purpose of publishing it was to present a chronicle of my difficulty coming to terms with my buried feelings and with the diagnosis of Parkinson's Disease in 1982 at a relatively young age 36. However, as the work progressed, another purpose began to emerge. Hence, this separate yet essential section was added.

I didn't want this "emerging" purpose to be left out or written into another book because I feel it is so important, especially for someone who has just been diagnosed with PD or another autoimmune disease. The point is that this book can be used as a bridge of communication between the victims of Parkinson's Disease and their doctors, i.e., general practitioner, neurologist, psychiatrist, psychologist, geriatrist etc., health care givers and their family members and friends. It can be used when it seems that doctors aren't able to see Parkinson's from a patient's point of view. This message attacks no one in the health care industry or any other industries. I hope you'll come to realize **we're all victims of victims** and **we're all in this together**.

When I was diagnosed with PD, I had worked ten years at an animal hospital. **This meant I was exposed to pesticides daily**. Wondering if these could be tied in with causing PD, I became interested in the research of Canadian Andre Barbeau. A friend gave me her collection of United Parkinson's Foundation newsletters. This source of information explained why he was studying nine hydrographic basins in Quebec. These areas had the highest incidence of PD in the country. <u>He thought that **herbicides** and **pesticides** from the surrounding forests draining into the population's water supply was the reason</u>. The question as to *why some people get PD and why others of the same exposure don't* was approached by Barbeau from the point of view of individual immune systems. Barbeau died before his research was finished. I did not understand the physiological process of pesticides on the nervous system, nor how close to the truth was my intuition leading me.

After ten years of denial and making adjustments to minimize the appearance of my condition, I started having serious episodes of being unable to manage everyday tasks due to weakness, abdominal pain, medication difficulties (dystonia, dyskinesia, and hypotension). I was also hospitalized three times. I was sent home with orders for 24 hour care and with the words of doom ringing in my ears: "you are in the latter stages of Parkinson's Disease...get your affairs in order..." I was angry! I was not ready to go! I had pulled out of low spots before in defiance of what doctors had told me and I had seen a <u>lot</u> of doctors, looking for some new approach to treatment. It angered me that they would make pronouncements without leaving any door open for **hope**. <u>No suggestion for making improvements for quality of life</u>. However, 'being written off for dead' meant that officially the door could be kicked open to the 'Natural' approach. Friends, upon hearing that I was dying, asked someone they knew if he would consider trying the 'Natural' approach with me - by way of looking at Parkinson's as being the result of chemical poisoning. He agreed. I'm curious if anyone else is having these dynamics in their life.

When we met, he told me he was a layperson studying this subject of chemical poisoning for better than two decades because he had a **birth defected child** and he wanted to know what **caused it** and **warn other parents. He uses accredited sources such as daily newspapers, books, magazines and periodicals etc., this way everyone could decide for themselves based on the facts.** In short, he never wanted any credit, he just needed to get this message out as soon as possible to stop the pain and suffering for everyone. He told me that there was a very simple way to view my condition: and that was to focus in on only one particular poison, because of its totally unique characteristics, and then asked if I was interested in tracking **Mercury Exposure** throughout my life. Over the past 5 years, he has brought me a chain of evidence and critical *life saving information* of which that; I wish I had known in 1982, compared to what I know now. I might have been able to lessen my suffering. He said, "<u>Eventually everyone will be diagnosed with some form of autoimmune disease irregardless of their age</u>."

Most people call him the Mercury Man (hereafter "**MM**"). He started showing me exposure after exposure to Methyl Mercury Vapor in our daily lives. When he brought me a video tape of the 1953 Mercury Poisoning of a fishing village in Minamata, Japan, I saw the elderly twisted and ravaged, blind, deaf and tremulous. I saw very young children who had lost their balance, their eyesight, their hearing, their ability to speak and then I saw a woman lying in a bed. Her arms and legs rapidly jerking back and forth and twisting. I also saw the "mad suicidal cats" of Minamata, shaking and mimicking Parkinson's patients. At this point, he mentioned to me that he saw a resemblance in the way "mad cats" and "mad cows" moved and struggled to maintain their balance. I knew then why he wanted me to view this so that I could see someone that was <u>definitely poisoned with Mercury</u> experiencing the same tremors I have. This opened my eyes to a new way of understanding what causes Parkinson's and many, many other autoimmune diseases. I would be remiss at this point if I did not acknowledge the late W. Eugene Smith and his wife Aileen M. and their painful ordeal and their incredible efforts to warn the world about

continued on page 76

Exposure

Becky Herdson 1985

Cold once more

    weary and alone

        my true fear

    is to be unalone

Will I ever emerge from the shadow

    side of the moon?

Passively I find ways # Introduction

    to affirm the self-rejection

        I fear

    the dark voice within

The wallflower only looks on at the dance

    - afraid of hope.

I believe that the issues of improved education and enlightened care of patients with Parkinson's Disease need to be addressed simultaneously with the search for cause and a cure. When these are discovered, there is going to be an overlap time for knowledge distribution and procedures to be taught. There is a growing population of PD patients and a new attitude about the management of this enigmatic condition is needed YESTERDAY!

Many married PD patients, especially if they are Young Onset (under 40 years of age when diagnosed), find themselves divorced and fighting the battle alone at a time of life usually considered the prime age of family-building and establishing a solid career. PD is an expensive "lifestyle": neurology specialists, CT scans, MRIs, Pharmaceuticals, mental health care, walkers, wheelchairs, hospital beds for home care, in-home healthcare, assisted living, occasional/permanent nursing home care, etc.

Singlepersons often have no advocate, which can be disconcerting when one finds oneself in a nursing home or in a hospitalized situation, where it is a shock to discover that most medical professionals know little about Parkinson's and have little understanding of the varying degrees of the varying needs of a PD patient. This often results in nurses and aides becoming irritable with inconsistencies and slow to respond due to a misperception that the patient is just being troublesome. Add to this mix that most of the drugs prescribed to those with Parkinson's are psychotropic (cause vivid and lucid dreaming and also hallucinations and drug induced schizophrenia).

In 1982, Parkinson's Disease was usually associated with an age group twenty or more years older than I.

Being diagnosed with PD at age 36 was unexpected. The symptoms were confusing both to me and my family. It became difficult to do my job. It was two years before a diagnosis was found. Some days would find me weaker or slower or more fatigued than others. About six months before it was decided that my illness was Parkinson's my husband announced he wanted a divorce. Suddenly, after ten years, I had no marriage and no job. I had a mysterious health problem. I was stunned. My life was unrecognizable.

After a few weeks, I began to realize that as I felt more relaxed and free each day, that I had been living with anxiety for a long time.

Fear is something we all have in common. We tend to hide our fears away, afraid of the reactions of others, viewing them as hindrances. When crisis strikes, however, fear can be magnified from hindrance to staggering obstacle. Usually attached to this obstacle is an opportunity for spiritual growth and self-awareness.

The series of artwork and poetry presented here is my record of therapy with a Jungian psychologist, who is also a Presbyterian minister. I had done very little artwork since graduating from college thirteen years earlier. I had allowed a vital part of my being to be ignored.

Working with my dreams was a helpful step for me. It became apparent that establishing emotional distance had become my way of relating. I feared rejection, and in my efforts to avoid rejection and to please others, I had no direction of my own. I had learned to conceal my feelings so well that they were hidden from myself. Drawing helped to access those feelings.

I gradually understood that having given up responsibility to choose for myself, I lived with the alternatives of dependence and compliance. I had followed fear to a place where powerlessness brought me denied anger and unrecognized depression. One day, it finally dawned on me that the medical name for PD, Paralysis Agitans, punctuated my psychological state. I was agitating to break free and immobilized at the same time. Today when my symptoms intensify, it is often a sign of discord, that fear has intruded.

Keeping one's life free of fear requires vigilance. When I falter (and I do!) in spite of self-judgment, my faith and hope in God somehow strengthen. Though this presentation is quite personal in nature, and as we each have our own path to follow, the struggle of the individual is a shared struggle, born of the longing to find meaning, to make sense of the events in one's life.

The self reflects
    opposites exact
and wonders why
        opposites
attract

Initial Shock

The drawings began when I had a dream of "opposites" in which a small airplane with a woman pilot was sitting on the beautiful white sands on the floor of a tropical ocean. There was a soft infusion of golden light through the clear pale blue water. Hearing the sound of an airplane overhead, she looked up through the water to see a fish flying through the air! At this point a symbol "flashed" and was gone. It was a circle, horizontally divided with a top half white and the lower half black, with an "S" in the center. My counselor said this kind of dream is not uncommon for people who are in crisis, trying to reconcile old belief systems with new realities.

It was suggested that I draw this symbol, and each day until the next session, I was to draw a circle and see what developed. The first pencil drawing was the result of the creative process at the end of the week. The picture is of a winged woman rising up and out of a stylized lily, under a full moon.

I refer to the process of drawing which developed from this time spent in therapy as "dreaming on paper." Drawing a circle first is a way to focus and to contain a composition that begins with a few lightly sketched lines, and something takes form.

Early on, an artist friend remarked that some of the drawings looked like Native American shields and recommended the book, "Seven Arrows", by Hyemeyohsts Storm, for information on shields. I found this interesting because my mother had told me that my great-great grandmother was a Native American named Missouri Ann.

As the Native American theme began to grow, at the suggestion of William Fetter, I showed my work to Navajo Dr. David Warren, who was retiring from the Bureau of Indian Affairs that year in Santa Fe, New Mexico. Fetter and Warren had both worked about a decade ago on a UNESCO project titled Technology, Arts and Cultural Transformations.

Dr. Warren selected several pictures which he felt were obvious in their Native American qualities.

2

All of Dr. Warren's selections were curious to me, being unexpected. For example, the picture of the woman emerging or floating from the deep dark center of the circle, (see picture with text "Brightness unbearable..." page 14 and 15) Dr. Warren said this was Southwest Native American, bringing to mind the "sipapu" or passage between worlds. His comments about Native American symbols in my work were humbling. He suggested that I come back to the Southwest to attend the dances, that it might be important to me. While it has not worked out for me to do so, I became very interested in learning about he dances and the Kachinas (Spirit dancers).

becky deitch hudson   may 1983

4

Softly

> *as the moonlit night*

she sighs

> *at her memory's unfolding*

and then

> *lifts her wings toward*

the warm night wind

> *to celebrate:*

She knows she is forever

Becky Hudson 1985

stepping into the vision
revelation of spirit
      finding the gift: a truth lost to
fear
wondering at myself
      losing what was never claimed
how can one lose what is inherent?

Becky Hudson
1985

8

One who is lifted

    into the wind

you touch freely

    what my soul

        cries for

And I am safe

    in the shadow

        of your wings

"A Fish Screaming" Mark Rubin
1-26-66

Becky Deitch Hudson
6-6-83

10

Screaming fish

    go away

An embodiment of denied anger and
fear

cuts through the confusion, shrieking

impotent rage into nothingness

    don't come back

        another day

    he's gone

        Oh God

    doesn't make sense

must be a bad dream

    he wouldn't

what did I do

        when I think of all

    how many times we

        this didn't happen

please God

    I couldn't have what the doctor

        no no no

    it's not fair

        it's not

11

The unknown is frightening
and dark and empty
and the known so familiar
Doesn't make sense anymore –
it has become the
unknown
How can something be formed
out of nothing?
Did we create God, or did he create
us?

Becky Hudson 1985

14

Brightness unbearable
darkness familiar

now, both places
you see
you are blind

Becky Hudson 1984

16

My grandmother

    *How I've wanted to see her
again, to talk with her, to feel
    the love and acceptance I have
not been able to give myself.*

the light
makes possible
the shadow

18

My disowned shadow
  I begin to trace
parts of myself
  I begin to face

19

Becky Hudson 1985

Consider of all things,

    the turtle.

It's slow, steady pace

    gives us heart

It's adaptable life

    takes our admiration

It's endurance

    encourages our faith

It's wisdom to take shelter

    advises us to reflect

It's self-containment

    exemplifies the centered life

It's noble qualities

    connect us with humility

then, consider of all things,

    connection

21

Becky Hudson 198:

22

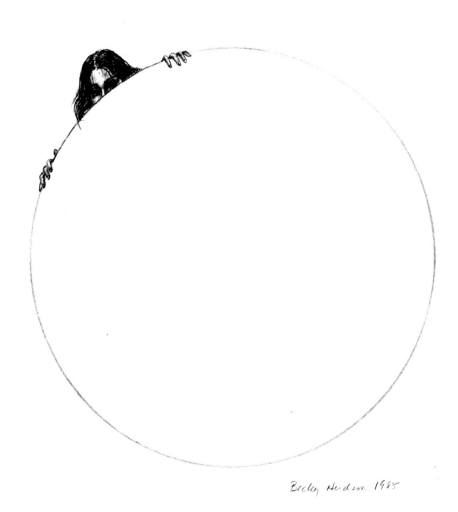

Becley Hudson 1985

Gravity secures the soul
Humor liberates it.

Mental and physical depression can overwhelm one's life. It seems to take twice the time and ten times the effort to perform ordinary tasks. Productivity becomes almost unknown, adding to the despair of the person afflicted. Attempting to force a positive attitude often ends in self-condemnation. All seems utterly hopeless.

I struggled with such depression for over a year and a half before I agreed to begin medication. I had stopped drawing during this time of denial, feeling trapped and frightened by my physical limitations. Medication helped physically and my mental attitude began improving.

Now I see depression as nature's way of recovery, as a dormancy that can be productive in its own time.

Dormancy

An angel on her deathbed lay
for love of each star fallen
"my heart is all and who I am"
you can hear her softly callin'

she's turned her face away from hope
can you hear her callin'?
"goodbye goodbye to my friends all
and salute each star that's fallen"

O Mother O Father extend your arms
the truth has pulled her under
the tower is by lightening struck
and the trumpets stilled by thunder

O One Whose Name is Not Revealed
Whose Lamb will slay the dragon
this angel cries herself to sleep
and prays she will awaken

And as she wanders in her sleep
hope reigns among the living
the heart that's true and often tried
knows and is forgiving

O angel sleeping in the dream
this truth remains unspoken
all sin is only God denied
His promise shines unbroken

Becky Hudson 1985

Is this what I have heard of – Purgatory?
I feel caught between life and death,
of what am I guilty that I must suffer here?
Did I bring this on myself?
What did I do?

 Please, Someone!

Becky Hudson 1985

ENOUGH!

Of what am I guilty?

Of self-hate: of playing God

27

Becky Hudson 1985

28

How did I confuse pacifism with passivism?

I misunderstood the teaching to "turn the other cheek." I thought it meant conflict-avoidance, denying feelings and pretending not to anger. Manipulating my way through life with a weak facade, I thought I was a victim who had no choice. This in itself was a choice to be helpless. I did not take responsibility for my choices (or seem to make any) for fear of criticism and being rejected, or of hurting someone else.

As said before, "keeping one's heartpath free of fear requires vigilance," and though I speak here in the past tense, I still do and most likely always will have to contend with this behavior.

A friend shared with me the definition he had adopted for God's love:

"Action taken in the best interest of."

He said he tried to make decisions that he had to make for himself and others who asked for his help, based on this definition.

Oh, yesterday's dream

return to me

wounded, I wait

My name is Broken Wing
I am Fallen-from-the-sky.

Becky Hudson 1985

32

Today's Pain,

Make me whole

wounded, I wait

A new name comes with healing

and colors come after the rain

Becky Hudson 1985

34

Tomorrow's Hope,

take form in the void

...I wait

My name is Rainbow Woman,
I am Colors-after-the-Rain.

I sat "doodling" at my drawing table. The two circles colliding startled me, one with linear structures piercing the other with a long spear, causing organic-like pieces to be torn away. The violence disturbed me. Well, here we go again, I thought. It had been about a year since I had moved into my own place to live, and had not done much art work.

I began drawing my usual pencil drawing. I let the urge for color lead me. I had collected some colored Design marking pens and colored pencils for doing art work for Church posters, etc. My first drawing disturbed me. It looked nightmarish and worse. The second drawing was also startling, as I began with a face and then using dots to build an image. I jumped when it suddenly appeared: a spider! I was not getting a good feeling about this process. Color and curiosity kept me going. Some thing new was emerging and I wanted to see what it was. Scary. Color. Red. Fire, blood, anger. Feelings...

Impact

fear keeps the truth within
within,
and the truth within
waits,

knowing

Impact Series

39

Sometimes I hear you calling
        faintly in dark silence
have you heard me answer
        there is no answer

have you seen me crying
        numbly in dark silence
do you know emotion
        having no emotion

afraid to be alone
        aching in dark silence
how could I forget you
        having nothing to recall

weightless and detached
        seeking in dark silence
do you know choice
        having no choice

fallen angel,
        you are brutally denied
        with tender regret

until you know at last
        shining in dark silence
Who it is that guides
        your return to innocence

becky hudson

41

gift of the spider's

chosen purpose

the once fearsome web

is your silver cord

to unravel

kirley hudson

43

Being more than minute
        against the universal
        backdrop

I am penetrated
        by awareness of dreaming
        who I am

becky hudson ©1987

45

Rooted passivism routed pacifism

and

holiness is

mismarked

appease making a peace breaking

and

wholeness is

marked missed

-   an unchanneled dreamer

serves critical Mass

47

The essence of communion

in a stained glass

moment

49

weightless and detached

       seeking in dark silence

I asked how to be free

      of fear –

the Way, he told me, is in

      knowing choice

51

The answer is

    not an academic assessment

    of a cross section of brain

the question is

    what happened to me

the search is

    mindblowing

becky hudson ©1987

53

Within an abysmal womb
        of my own imagining
the wish to be born labors
        over the fear of birth

without my imagining
        the mountain calls
with its stillness and peace:
        "What's mine is yours"

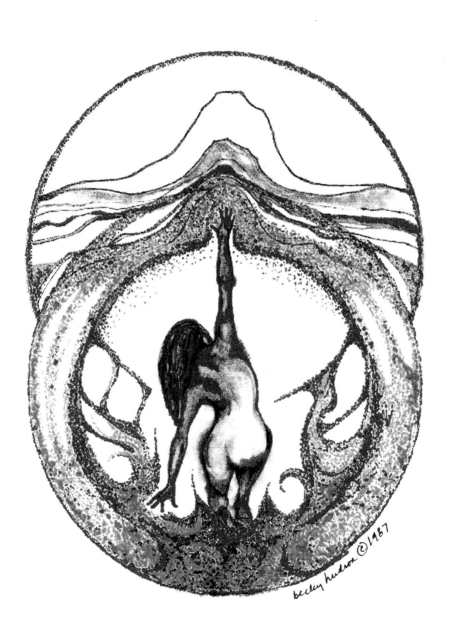

becky hudson ©1987

55

A picture worth

    two words –

metaphorical metamorphosis

becky hudgon 1997

And for the abstract colloquial
"out of synch":

Correctional – Emotive
Karmic Logic

What goes up comes down
What comes down goes up
What comes up goes down
What goes down comes up

in other words,
what comes down
goes down

becky hudson 1987

59

Pondering Soul

    hate not darkness –

    nor make it welcome

Wondering Soul,

    seek the sound –

    listen to the light

becky mudd 1987

61

insight

      in sight

63

content to be helpless
        I chose not to face
                the truth within and
        the inbetween place

then, choosing freedom
        I moved to embrace
                a choice born of fear
        and irrational haste

deprived of compassion
        the same path I trace
                choosing again
        the inbetween place

full of compassion
        the truth within waits
                my unknowing choice
        is suspension of grace

becky hudson ©1987

becky hudson

65

choice becomes knowing

  transfearence begins

Dream visitor

a silent messenger
      enters twilight
      finding me

where pretenders
      sleepwalk cautiously
      in veiled pallor

and then
      takes the raven's form
      reminding me

the inbetween
      place of unchoosing
      has no color

69

celebrate sunrise

    the truth within sings

        may the colors of

daybreak

    shine on your wings

we are God's children

    entrusted to live for Him

        flying on faith that

    he wants us to bring

so all those who see us

    will also believe in Him

        sharing the rainbow

    that shines on our wing

Breaking Through

You are known
you are the knowing
of the journey in the night
that is for touching lost ones
found sleeping in the light

you are gifted
you are the giving
of a present full of laughter
that is for healing worry
about before and after

you are love
you are loving
full of empty and content
you give your name to others
and your name is Blessing Sent...

"Innocence"

I looked for this word in the dictionary following a dream in which there was an elderly couple. Elders in one's dream-life usually represent the wise ones within. The only other recollection from the dream was a key phrase that I had written down when I awakened from the dream. (If I was too sleepy to record the dream, the key phrase would sometimes help me recall more, later.)

The key phrase was "return to innocence." The meaning I found in the dictionary for the word "innocence" was: acting without guile or cunning.

We are born innocent, helpless and dependent.

Perhaps the dream was a comment on how the innocent are introduced to fear as a way to control and be controlled. Then as awareness develops that choices are serious responsibilities. If one feels remorse or guilt from harm done to others, and if one wishes to change, to be reborn, he may choose to "return to innocence" by making a choice to act without guile and cunning.

As a young girl, I would often ask questions or talk about certain topics with my grandparents rather than my parents. I miss being able to talk with them.

I have often wondered if the negative events in our lives are not given to us by God, as I have heard people say, but used by him to perfect us. My father had Alzheimer's, and as he began to lose short term memory more and more, everything was always new and the best and the most and he delighted in that. It was a tough time for our family, but we often speak of this stage of transition with great fondness. It was a tough time for him also, of course, and he got through with his sense of humor. One of the cards my mother received from friends after my father's passing mentioned a gathering of many old friends and that my parents attended. Dad was not able to recognize and remember most of the people, and it embarrassed him…but he said as he left the party, "This is the best bunch of strangers I've ever known."

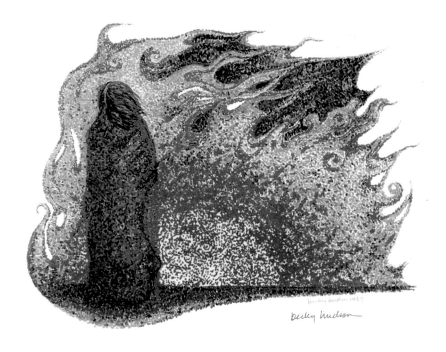

Becky Hudson

One more person discovers that there is life after diagnosis, after shattering crisis, after the crushing disappointment of the fall of a dream.

No matter the specifics or to what degree, we share this experience of "crisis," and it has been said for thousands of years that the crises in our lives often open the way for blessings and opportunities.

Being wounded, we are vulnerable, which is a state we spend a lot of time avoiding, dubbing it negative. I had occasion to look for the word "vulnerable" in a dictionary. One definition was "Capable of being wounded."

There is strength to be found in our vulnerability. We begin to recognize each other; our compassion is the honor we receive.

Epilogue

"What Would It Mean If Mercury Caused Parkinson's?"
(Continued)

Mercury Poisoning in their book Minamata. Minamata leads one to a whole new understanding of all autoimmune diseases.

Next, he showed me the October, 1972 issue of National Geographic. The article was titled **"Mercury: Man's Deadly Servant, Quicksilver and Slow Death." "From Japan Comes A Dire Warning"** referring to Minamata's massive Mercury Poisoning.

This is just a brief excerpt from the article: **"Metal's 20th-Century Uses Are Legion.** ....And so, as man moved into the modern technological age, Mercury moved with him. By 1969 world production reached some 20 million pounds and one industry expert counted more than 3,000 different uses for the element. Dentists have long used a **50-percent Mercury** amalgam in tooth fillings. The Mercury dissolves an alloy of silver and tin, and this compound solidifies on application. Last year [1968], more than 160 million such fillings went into American teeth. The next document I saw was the 1997 Material Safety Data Sheet *(M.S.D.S.)*, warning of poisonous side effects from *Mercury vapor that continuously off gasses for the life of the filling that result in central nervous system damage*, which was issued by Dentsply/Caulk, the manufacturer of Mercury amalgam fillings for the American Dental Association. It was founded 150 years ago on the *'fatally flawed thinking'* that *Mercury is a safe poison for use in the oral cavity.* They still defend the safety of Mercury to this day and have the support of all public health agencies. He then brought me a copy of The Environmental Magazine a.k.a. "E". The May/June, 2002 issue. The cover reads: **"Got Mercury? This Toxic Heavy Metal is in TUNA and SWORDFISH, VACCINES, DENTAL FILLINGS, and in our AIR and WATER. It's Time We Got It Out."** To counter Dr. Abe Lieberman's statement "Mercury isn't a Cause of Parkinson's Disease." **MM** pointed out Dr. James Parkinson and his patients were exposed to Mercury Vapor from coal burning back in 1817, just as we are now in 2004. see: www.whonamedit.com

A front page story in USA Today, Nov. 5, 2002, reads: **"People who eat a lot of fish may run health risk. Study finds elevated consumption can lead to high intake of Mercury."** Another front page story in a USA Today paper, dated Aug. 6, 2003, reads: **"Frantic search is on for memory-loss cures. Scientist find answers to why old and young Americans struggle to remember; dementia crisis may be on horizon.** Toll on families: Dianne McLain, 55, an L.A. DENTIST, hopes her stimulating life-and new research-will prevent her daughter Caitlin, 12, from suffering with dementia, which has struck her mother, Janet, 77." **MM** – If Diane is an **A**.merican **D**.ental **A**.ssociation member, she will violate her code of ethics to warn her mother or patient about the *M.S.D.S.* sheets which list Mercury's Poisonous devastation to major organs, etc., making Janet and Caitlin victims of 'uninformed consent' due to the psychiatric symptoms of Mercury poisoning, proving **'there is no one to blame.' Everyone is just a victim of a victim.** If Diane was in her 'Natural Mind,' she would have never purposely poisoned the ones she loves the most.

Citing the University of Calgary, Dept. of Physiology & Biophysics, Faculty of Medicine, F. L. Lorsheider, C. C-W. Leong and N.I. Syed produced a video on

Mar. 26, 2001, **"How Mercury Causes Brain Neuron Degeneration."** **MM** - These researchers did not let Mercury blind them. Their research clearly concluded: '**Only Mercury does cause Alzheimer's**'. Seattle Post Intelligencer (hereafter, "P.I".), Nov. 15, 2002, **"Silver (Mercury Amalgam) fillings for kids safe, government affirms."** Seattle Times, July 2, 2003, **"A diet full of fish could mean a diet full of Mercury."**

The 60 Minutes Broadcast, Dec. 1990, **"Is There Poison In Your Mouth."** In the introduction to the program, Morley Safer holds up a Mercury amalgam filling and says, "Because it's been around so long and because it was assumed that the Mercury was made stable when mixed with other metals, *Amalgam fillings* (Mercury) *were never tested for safety*. One of those 'remedies' the Food and Drug Administration automatically approved. *But now, a growing number of scientists, doctors' and dentists' are saying silver (Mercury) amalgams should be banned.*"

P.I., Sept. 1, 2003, reads: **"States found deficient in MENTAL CARE for CHILDREN."** **MM** - Our '**fatally flawed thinking**' is easily pointed out and makes it clear why our children are now suffering psychiatric disorders and neurological diseases that only used to show up in the adult population. Today's children have ever increasingly higher Methyl Mercury levels. USA Today, May 29, 2003: **"Suffer the little children in the search for cures"**. **MM** - Isn't the cure for cancer to stop *manufacturing SIN*thetic carcinogens? Time Magazine, Aug. 19, 2002, **"Inside the Volatile World of the Young and Bipolar. Why are so many kids being diagnosed with the disorder once known as MANIC DEPRESSION?"** Time Magazine, Nov. 3, 2003, **"Are We Giving Kids TOO many DRUGS?"** A medicated generation is growing up with quick fixes for mood and behavior. Here are the benefits-and risks." **MM** - Combining critical research, now, can give laypeople and professionals a better way to profile the Bicameral Brain (hereafter BB) without judging the person, but rather only the *malfunctions* their BB is manufacturing.

At www.relfe.com/wernickes_self_sabotage.html, Stephanie Relfe posted this comment about Julian Jaynes' research: "Experiments have shown that if the Wernicke's in the left half of the brain is electrically stimulated during speech, it will interfere with the ability to talk properly, almost halting speech. The same type of stimulation to the Wernicke's area in the right brain, however, causes a person to hear "voices" or "commands". These are usually of an authoritarian or dictatorial nature, and can be identified as the voice of **one who was feared, admired** or "**looked up to**" by the person being stimulated. We call these commands 'Wernicke's commands,' because they are commands stored in the Wernicke's area of the brain."

MM - Many people are now re-examining Julian Jaynes' research but may have been blind to the fact that the installation of Mercury amalgam tooth fillings in your mouth is the equivalent of installing batteries in your brain. Your saliva acts as the electrolyte. It's the equivalent of installing a *Doomsday Chip* in the brain of a computer. Couldn't the fillings in our mouths be providing the constant electrical power supply needed for the BB? *Wouldn't this restrict our free will*?

The BB will **insulate** and **isolate** key pieces of information to keep mankind trapped in his **Methyl Mercury Matrix**. The quickest way **back to reality** is to realize as laypeople and professionals, that we now have a simple understanding of how **Mercury devastates** our 'Natural Mind's Abilities'. Could Julian Jaynes, author of *The Origin of Consciousness and the Breakdown of the Bicameral Mind,* have solved the age old mystery of why mankind believes, thinks, murders and acts the way he does, *never ever being able to learn from any of his mistakes?* Could this be the source of the on board power supply that creates the BB? Located on www.algonet.se/~leif/FUSCIFCT.html "Scientifically Proven Facts About Mercury: (41) <u>Amalgam fillings produce electrical currents which might be injurious to health</u>. These currents are measurable in Micro Amps. The Central Nervous System (Brain) operates in the range of Nano-Amps this is One Thousand times less than a Micro Amp. **MM -** <u>Giving new meaning to being amped up</u>." Jaynes' BB research becomes even more understandable when linked to Dr. Jaro Pleva's research profiling Mercury's intoxicating influence over the "Mood and Behavior" of the 'Natural Mind' creating the BB. He asks, *Does Mercury Make Dentists Mad?* and *Are Promoters of Dental Amalgam Poisoned by Mercury?*

Applying both Jaynes' and Pleva's findings to Dr. Helen Caldicott's book: *The New Nuclear Danger: George W. Bush's Military Industrial Complex.* **MM -** If she applied the BB profile to her *<u>clinical paranoia diagnosis*,</u>* coupled with her astute observations makes it easy to see the *split in consciousness* between the constant *'death wish'* Mercury's voice induces within the BB and the opposite wish that *'all survive'* generated by the 'Natural Mind'. <u>Based on the evidence you've just read, to this point, isn't it time we find mankind not guilty due to his insanity which makes him commit crimes against his own humanity</u>?

becky - "I feel questioning the answer Dr. Lieberman gave to this letter writer could change the way we understand medicine. I ask this most important question again, "Why not Mercury, Dr. Lieberman?"
From: AskTheDoctor

"A letter writer cited an outbreak of Mercury Poisoning in Japan where the symptoms resembled Parkinson Disease. This occurred when polyvinyl was being discharged into Minamata Bay. [note: the writer of the original letter that appeared in the Wall Street Journal mistakenly stated Polyvinyl Mercury instead of Methyl Mercury] Dr. Lieberman's response: "First the **fish** were poisoned, then the animals **(cats)** and the people who ate the contaminated fish. <u>The cats and people (some of whom I examined) developed a disorder **distinctly different** from Parkinson's Disease</u>."

MM -You have to ask yourself what it is that Dr. Lieberman isn't seeing when we see clearly that Minamata's Mercury-poisoned people act and look strikingly like people with Parkinson's in America. Many doctors traveled to Minamata like Dr. Lieberman, trying to figure out what was causing the 'strange disease'. They would leave puzzled as to the cause. Could Dr. Lieberman along with the other doctors have been Blinded Bicamerally? When you turn to the back of the Minamata book, on page 182 of the Medical Report, figure 3: "Pathological findings were as follows: "Lesions in the cerebral cortex: <u>Neurons</u> of the cerebral cortex were generally damaged. The calcarine regions of the occipital lobe, the precentral cortex of the frontal lobe and the postcentral cortex of the parietal lobe were especially severely damaged. In acute cases, **the cerebral cortex becomes**

spongy." **MM** - Dr. Lieberman needs to see the breakthrough **400th cat experiment** of Dr. Hosokawa, which proved conclusively, **only Mercury** could cause the **'strange disease'** to occur. Is it a coincidence <u>Alzheimer's has a trademark spongy brain</u> much like **"madd cows"**? Why couldn't **"madd cats"**, **"madd cows"**, **"madd fish"** and **"madd man's"** brain damage *all* be caused by Mercury Poisoning?

Dr. Lieberman: "While the person who wrote the letter cited Parkinson's Disease in a young dentist who handled Mercury amalgams, there is no higher incidence nor prevalence of Parkinson's Disease among dentists than among other professionals: accountants, doctors, lawyers. And youth is not a barrier in Parkinson's Disease as illustrated by the occurrence of Parkinson's Disease in Michael J. Fox.

"I wish I knew the cause of Parkinson's Disease so we could get rid of it, *Mercury, however, is not the cause.*" Abe Lieberman, MD, Medical Director, NPF, Professor of Neurology, University of Miami School of Medicine, askthedoctor@www.parkinson.org

becky - *"I wish it could be that simple. For instance, what if Mercury DOES cause PD – or factor into the cause in a major way, what then? How easy would it be to get rid of such a deadly and complex substance?"*

MM - What if Dr. Lieberman would look at Michael J. Fox's dental history first, and applied the protocol to all his patients; *he would start tracking a pattern of autoimmune disease occurring after Mercury amalgam fillings were installed.* The young dentists' Parkinson's diagnosis fits his occupational exposure to Mercury. Your BB profile of anyone is not complete unless you have their **dental=mental** records. This is important if you are going to be judged by people in authority such as: Emperors, **Czarrs**, Doctors, Judges, Lawyers, Police, Presidents, Priests, Psychiatrists, Teachers, etc. *It doesn't matter to Mercury whose brain it takes over and destroys.*

From the 1990, 60 Minutes, CBS News interview:
"Is There Poison In Your Mouth?"

Dr. Vimy: "This issue is <u>chronic exposure low dose</u> to a **heavy metal**. And <u>our laboratory is the entire human population in the western world who has amalgams, and no one has really looked at that aspect of Mercury Exposure.</u> *A great deal is known about acute exposures. One time, two time large exposures, but this is something that people have day after day after day. And we're just at the beginning of that trail of investigation."*

Morley Safer: "According to *Goodman and Gilman* **there have been epidemics of Mercury Poisoning that we've misdiagnosed for years.** The reasons for the tragic delays, says this text book, include <u>vagueness of early clinical signs and the medical professionals unfamiliarity with the disease.</u>"

Dr. Zann: "It is said clearly **doctors very rarely make a diagnosis of Mercury Poisoning** because of the difficultness of it. It comes in different phases. One has headaches. One has tiredness. One has this and one has that. <u>It's a very difficult diagnosis for one to make especially when it's Micro Mercurialism,</u> *very small amounts.* **MM** - Dr. Zann wisely notes everyone can suffer totally different symptoms.

We interrupt our message with two <u>Breaking News Bulletins</u> which will help make our point easily understandable: **Keiko** died Dec. 12, 2003. Dec. 24, 2003, Seattle P. I. - **"Mad-cow disease hits state; feds say beef 'absolutely safe.' First Case Found Near Yakima, Wa."** Seattle Times, Dec. 20, 2001, "Fossils indicate whales' kinship to hippos and cows." **MM** - Could both the orcas and the cows be sending mankind the same message regarding his **M.A.D.D.**ness (**M**.utually **A**.ssured **D**.eath and **D**.estrruction)?

"Mad Cows or Mad Scientist? The Suppression of Alternative Explanations" by David Crowe, reads: "One man, Mark Purdey, has turned himself from organic dairy farmer into an amateur scientist and globe-trotting epidemiologist to doggedly continue building the major alternative theory: *BSE-like diseases were found in Colorado among deer and elk in an area of the front ranges where overpopulation often forced starving animals to graze on pine needles.* These showed very high levels of Manganese, perhaps due to acid rain from upwind smelters. In Iceland, Purdey found Scrapie associated with similar high Manganese/low Copper soil conditions. In Slovakia the two clusters of CJD are close to ferromanganese factories and glassworks (heavy users of Manganese). These cases may well be related to the almost eradicated occupational disease known as "Manganese Madness" which occurred among miners exposed to poorly ventilated working conditions. Its symptoms and brain pathology are similar to spongiform encephalopathy's." (source: www.mercola.com /2002/aug/10/mad_cow.htm)."

MM - The BB will suppress *All* alternatives to its own M.A.D.D.ness. Mark didn't realize the pine needles had to contain high levels of Mercury due to **coal burning**. If the brains of the deer and elk are spongy, couldn't it only be caused by Mercury?

Minamata Medical Report page 181 and 182 answers the manganese question: "At first manganese was suspected. Then selenium. Then thallium. Although large amounts of these poisons were detected in the environment and in autopsied patients, experiments with cats showed that none of these substances produced the same symptoms as the "strange disease."....Experiments were begun on the possibility that the causal element was a combination of several poisons. Results, however, were negative. Researchers began experiments with Methyl Mercury. Cats who were fed Methyl Mercury directly showed the same symptoms as those cats affected with Minamata Disease after eating the fish and shellfish of Minamata Bay."

MM - Mark's great research needs to be linked with another layperson's findings if we're going to 'S.ave O.urS.elves'. Howard Lyman, "the 'madd cowboy', was interviewed on the Coast-to-Coast (hereafter "C-T-C") talk radio show by host George Noory on Jan. 7, 2004. Howard says....."the symptoms are almost identical to Alzheimer's and if you look at the U.S., we claim, right now, in the U.S., that we have 4 million cases of Alzheimer's, but when they examined two cases I know of, the Pittsburgh Veteran's Study and Yale study where they actually took the brains of demented people who died and looked at them under the microscope. They found anywhere from 6-13% of them that were diagnosed with dementia, with Alzheimer's, really had the human form of "madd cow" disease. Our government basically says "we have one case of CJD per million inhabitants". That means we have 270 people in the U.S. that should have CJD.

80

But if we look at those studies from 6-13% misdiagnosed - 4 million cases out there - we have a whole lot more people out there that have diseases that are not being diagnosed than what anybody wants to admit."

A C-T-C listener, Rick, called in during the interview and asked: "First off, I'm outraged because I'm listening to this and I'm saying to myself, maybe I'm contaminated. *I'm 49 years old. My liver is going to crap and I have diabetes.* My immune system is somewhat low and I'm thinking - could my diet over the decades, have contributed to this? And also I was thinking we're concerned, right now, the country's concerned, about terroristic threats. *Things happening inside this country by outsiders and it never ceases to amaze me what Americans do to Americans, sometimes exceeding what any terrorist from outside can do to us.* My question is: and this is the cynical piece operating, these forces that are out here controlling the meat industry, they're very powerful. **They have a lot of money behind them.** It doesn't seem like anything can happen. **It doesn't seem like the people have any voice in this anymore.** How can we change this? It seems entrenched. **MM** - To help Rick and everyone else understand what we've done, due to our brain damage, we followed *SIN*thetic Scientific Technologies. What if the vast majority of 'downer cows' are suffering from Mercury Poisoning with no *prion* present? The BB is always based on **greed** or **gold fever**, which mentally manifests itself as a *'poison-for-profit'* syndrome. Seattle P. I., Jan. 4, 2004: **"USDA dominated by industry it regulates."** In the P-I Opinion" section it reads: **"Economics drives industry reforms."** Newsweek, Mar. 23, 2001, "**The Slow Deadly Spread of Mad Cow Disease - How it could become an Epidemic."** Published in 1963 or 1964: "Shocking Results of Govt. Studies Reveal...Everyone in US is Being Poisoned by Mercury, written by Harold Martin from TODAY'S HEALTH published by the American Medical Association.

MM - Here are more typical Bicameral 20th Century farming practices that would create "madd cows": The National Police Gazette, Vol. CLXIX No. 9, Oct. 1964, **"GUARD YOUR HEALTH - How U.S. Agriculture Dept. Put CANCER in Your MILK,** by George McGrath. Insecticides and Cancer....."The astronomical increase in cancer among children." Seattle Times, 5 part series starting July 3, 1997, "Fear in the Fields, How Hazardous Wastes become Fertilizer. Spreading **heavy metals** on farmland is perfectly legal."

Channel 5, Jan. 15, 2004, the 5 pm news broadcast reports: *Washington state health officials* say: **"PCB levels are not high enough for them to issue any warning about salmon consumption** and they argue that the health benefits out weigh the risks.....As for exact consumption warning from the health department, they say they do not agree with what some of the people are saying out there, and **if you're (the public) expecting to get guidelines from the state health department on how much salmon you should eat, DON'T.** *They're not going to touch this.* Reporting live from Seattle, Wa. Gary Chittam". **MM** - *Mercury levels are always high enough to out weigh any health benefit from eating salmon or other fish!* What if our officials follow their own guidelines, **believing Mercury has a 'safe' level** because they're suffering from the **'poison-for-profit'** syndrome. Wouldn't the brains of the vast majority of Health and Human Services personnel be demented? What if their expertise, we trust in, is due to spongy brain? *Isn't this how the BB's thinking controls life on earth from birth to death?*

The Seattle P.I., July, 30, 2001, "**Mercury: Warning would cost too much. Those most at risk for eating Mercury-tainted fish are young children, whose developing brains and nervous systems are particularly susceptible to poisoning by the heavy metal.**" Seattle Times, Mar. 17, 2004, "**EPA let Industry (=Business) dictate policy on Mercury..... Mercury Rule** was **Political Creation**, staffer's say."

Seattle P. I., Feb. 5, 2004, "**Mercury Risk to Newborns Alarming**....New data from the **EPA doubles the estimate exposed in the womb**. About 630,000 children are born each year at risk for **Lowered Intelligence**. That nearly **doubles the previous EPA estimate**." **MM** - Haven't we all been poisoned by Mercury in utero for eons? These headlines explain why our children are Alcohol, Ecstasy and Methamphetamine users. This is why Preschoolers are on Ritalin, Zoloft, Paxil, Prozac and other S.S.R.I.'s. They're born only thinking and believing ***non*-Human or Bicamerally.**

Seattle P. I., Mar. 23, 2004, "**Science and medicine. FDA urges suicide warning on many anti-depressants'**. Seattle Times, Mar. 26, 2004, "**Army Seeks to Curb High Suicide Rate in US Troops in Iraq**". **MM** - We program our fatally flawed thinking into our children's brains as we were generation after generation.

The Orcas' Healing Project is closer to reality because of this program: On the night of **May 15, 2004,*1** Richard C. Hoagland, Art Bell's most familiar guest, brought David Wilcox on with him. They made profound announcements to the 20 million global family listeners. The full text can be found on Richard's website: enterprisemission.com. This is the Orcas' attempt to **super simplify** a very **complex message** regarding our immediate survival/fate. Did the BB's frequency weapons of warr destroy the intricate balance of the solar system and the 'Garden of Eden's 'Natural' Wave Form Frequency? **RH** - The solar system [in this Model] that we're living in, is a "**broken solar system**" following the **Catastrophe, the Warr** ...that resulted in the disappearance of "the guys on Mars" ... who, eventually, were a tiny fragment of "US" that appeared *HERE* (Earth).

MM - BB weapons of warr always intend to control or destroy any 'Life Force Frequencies.' Richard's research also points to the problem of an instant physical pole shift of the earth any time. He feels the only solution is to use the C-T-C family of listeners and their *'group consciousness'* to survive the *'flip'* making a *smooth non-catastrophic transition.* **Gold** mining always funds the Emperor/King's BB evil Empires, causing a catastrophic poisoning of Earth's waters with M.A.D.D.ness.

QUICKSILVER GALLEONS – Nat'l Geographic, Dec. 1979, by M. Peterson....A cargo essential to the Spanish Empire. Quicksilver-was used to amalgamate gold and silver from New World ore. But the 1724 shipment....perished in a hurricane. Bearing 400 tons of the King's Royal MERCURY. Without the MERCURY, even today worth almost three million dollars, Spanish bullion production feel off, convulsing the already shaky empire.

82

MM - He who controls the **gold** always creates the BB **God** belief systems, morals, laws, punishments, etc. Mercury is more precious than **gold** to any Holy Royal Corporate Royal Governmental/Commercial Empire.

Source: lonestar.texas.net/~robison/mercuralis.html:…Mercury is a Roman God, also known as the God of trade, profit and commerce. His temple on the Circus Maximux Aventine Hall was built in 495 BC. On **May 15*1** the Mercuralia was held in his honor. Merchants sprinkled water from his **sacred well** near Porta Capena on their heads. **They offered prayers to Mercury,** who in legend had been a thief, for forgiveness for past and future perjuries, for profit, and for the continued ability to cheat customers! The attributes of Mercury are the caduceus (a staff with two intertwined snakes; A.M.A. logo) and a purse (a symbol of his connection with commerce). **MM** - Isn't the warr machine really just a Complex Corporate Industrial Empire, above all?

USA Today, June 9, 2004, Gettysburg: Sam Newland of the "**U.S. Army Warr College…….**" Execs learn military lessons in leadership. **Military a model for execs. Sometimes, the lesson is what not to do.** The military itself is *quick* to point out that wartime decisions have been far from perfect and that lessons come just as often from wartime blunders as they do from brilliance. **MM** – Our warr **Trick**nology and, HUMAN de-evolution exploded with the installation of the **Quicksilver fillings** 150 years ago. **The first Warr Department employees moved in to the Pentagon on April 29, 1942** (see the history channel "History of the Pentagon"). **MM** – Wouldn't the employees have to be mentally demented after decades of carrying out warrs under the influence of Mercury Vapor? The Pentagon interior was undergoing a 15 year Mercury and Asbestos removal on 9/11. It's all new *SIN*thetic interior will off gass even more Mercury vapor, i.e., plastics etc.

Source: **International Movement to Ban Mercury (Hg),** Nov. 2, 2001, www.mercurypolicy.org. "The Pentagon balked at a plan…..to have the Defense Dept. accept excess Mercury from a **Main Chlor-Alkali facility** into **its existing stockpiles of Weapons Grade Mercury** housed at four sites across the country."

Seattle P.I., June 10, 2004, Nation – "**U.S. to destroy its deadliest chemical**," AP.– A Cold War-era concoction so lethal it could kill untold millions…was produced…as a doomsday deterrent, by Rick Callahan. **MM** – The BB will see self-extinction as the 'only solution.'

"The Emperor Wears No Clothes: The Authoritative Historical Record of Cannabis and the Conspiracy Against Marijuana – by Jack Herer. (hereafter, **T.E.W.N.C.**) Popular Mechanics Magazine, June 1939 "From Test Tube to You" by Lammot DuPont. **MM** – Did Lammot DuPont's BB appoint him **god,** reinvent*er* of the 'Garden of Eden' out of *Un*-Natural man-made plastics and create pesticides to extinct 'Natural'– Cannabis to protect his *Patented Petrochemical Pharmaceutical Profits Empire?*

THE HISTORY CHANNEL PRESENTS
PLASTICS ON THE MARCH

Narrator: "They have taken over and transformed our world molding themselves into an infinity of products invading every space including outer space and the human heart. Now plastics, test tube materials have quite literally changed the substance of our lives.

WE HAD ENTERED THE PLASTICS AGE

MM - Roman Emperors are now diagnosed *clinically paranoid**, schizophrenic, bipolar and suicidal. Couldn't this change how we view Christ's *crucifixion?* Couldn't the Emperors have suffered from Alzheimer's like President Reagan suffered with while in power? Alzheimer's can't be diagnosed early enough, but the BB's fatally flawed thinking *is*, now, easy to see.

Source: Bill Moyers **"Trade Secrets** REAGAN INAUGURATION NARRATION: **Ronald Reagan was petrochemical's favorite Presidential candidate."** The Reagan team asked *BUSINESS* for a wish-list of actions that could be completed within the first 100 days. In less than a third of that time, the new **President signed an executive order** that 'transformed' the 'battle' over *the safety of chemicals*. **MM** – Now Mercury has *more* rights than human beings.

Seattle, P.I., July 2, 2004, front page, **"I don't really feel anger yet. 'I know I will'** – *Lead dangers stun parents*. Schools should have told them of *tainted water, they say*."

MM – Richard happily verifies the C-T-C *audience saved his life* after his heart attack. David revealed Russian Research finds replicas of the 'Great Pyramid' have 'healing abilities'. **Now its decision time 2004**. Will you continue to follow the M.A.D.D. Hatter's scientific **groupacide** or will some of us combine what little is left of our Mercury 'Impaired Individual' 'Natural Mind's Abilities' with the Orcas' to **S.O.S.**?

Seattle, P.I., Mar. 5, 2004, P.I. Opinion – **"Science Should Dictate Orca Plan"**. Luna's **(POV)** says *no* because **E=MC2** = *A*.rtificial *Un-I*.ntelligence generated by Alzheimer's or spongy brain. The Hopi word Koyonnasquatsi (see video), means life-out-of-('Natural') balance. The *'mind disappears'* when Mercury randomly electrif$r$ies and destroys its infinite electronic 'balancing frequency'.

AP, July 12, 2003, **"Bush Ups attacks on Marijuana. Asks court to OK doctor penalties,"** by Gina Holland: **MM** - Was Jesus silenced by the Emperor because he was trying to remind mankind his Mind has Miraculous 'Natural Abilities' and that **Gold** was a false **God**, unlike the sacred-essential 'Life Mind Frequency Force' found in the 'Natural Golden Green Cannabis Plant' found in Mother Earth's 'Garden of Eden'? The *Only Cure for Cancer*: stop living from test tube to you. **Because mankind outlawed Cannabis, he'll *never* come close to seeing 2012.** USA Today, July 7, 2003, front page, **"Bush Pushes For New Nukes and testing."**

MM - The picture of a U.S. Army doctor looking in the mouth of Saddam Hussein (2003), is a powerful image/message for mankind that both men are under the same intoxicating 'fog of warr', because there is no reasoning with or stopping the BB's 'death wish.' It must be 'healed remotely.' *No civilization has ever 'saved' itself from Mercury's 'resonant frequency of evil.'* Thus, the BB is the ultimate W.M.D and man the ultimate **warr head**. Seattle P.I., Aug. 8, 2003, **"Groups sue to stop Navy from using sonar, fearing harm to mammals."** Seattle P.I., Nov. 8, 2003, **"Wider Use of Sonar Approved by House."** MM –

The BB is going to **'flip'** the final switch and we're all going to be playing H.A.A.R.P's. It's always a **_divine_** man-made-dead-end invention that will result in no **'_Day after Tomorrow._'**

June 16, 2004, **"Canada Scientists Try to Move Killer Whale."** A group of local Indians were opposing the scientists' efforts, saying they believe the whale (**Luna**) is the reincarnation of their late chief.

Luna - On **June 22, 2004,***2 Mattie Stepanek was laughing and playing on Keikos back when they were spotted breaching over the top of the 'Great Pyramid'. They are telling everyone they've touched. You're not alone. Mattie's message is more urgent than ever. He showed us how poisons from **all** the world's warr machines **kill** far more children then its **bullets** will. Was Mattie feeling warr had destroyed **all** children's 'Natural Heartsong Frequency' feelings of love, play and happiness? Here is Mattie's feelings assembled out of context: Mattie - (Future of Life? Warr and Hatred). (We the People, We cannot win), (Signal or Symbol, Most people believe), (Children live what they learn. When I was a baby). (**About death...isn't it odd**)?

Luna and Mattie are warning again that from birth to death we are BB programmed that **warr** is the **only** solution being started over meaningless BB ego-symbols sewn onto **SIN**thetic rags bearing the Emperor's _Holy Royal_ corporate _logo_. **Isn't it odd to die for nothing? MM** - Burning oil destroys life. Warr runs on burning oil spreading Mercury Vapor.

Mattie - **About Happiness,** To me Happiness is traveling. **Not really "me" traveling, But my Heartsongs traveling.** When the songs in my heart, **Travel out and around the world.** In the things that I say and, In the poems and stories that I write, And in the prayers that **_I feel to God_**, And when the letters and words, Of those Heartsongs bring some **Peace to the countries and people,** **_Who have warr in their lives,_** That is real happiness, To me. _Mattie J.T. Stepanek_

Luna - Children and adults stop feeling because warr/terror is too painful/deadly. Your self-contained Heartsong Healing/Feeling Frequencies only work when you, '_feel_' loved, safe and secure. Only Heart Felt Play, Love and Laughter automatically generate your Heartsongs to 'Heal Our Garden of Eden'.

June 22, 2004*2, "**Lone orca escapes after reported captured.**" Gold River, British Columbia - Like something out of a movie, Luna the lonely killer whale, has apparently escaped. **MM** – These two events on **June 22, 2004*2**, announce: the re-emergence of the 'Natural Mind's Sacred Indigenous' **_consciousness_** which will help **_all_** of 'Mother Earth's children.

Luna is throwing us **_the_** Final Life Preserver. J, K and L pods contacted you, Art, and your listeners, approximately 5 years ago. Remember when your guest Dr. Randall Eaton discussed the Orcas' 'Healing Abilities'? You also felt they were contacting us. This caller clearly understands their message: "I'm calling from California. First of all I had a very powerful dream about the whales and the message to us was: to get in touch with the whales directly. But what I want to share with you comes out of a medicine wheel teaching of the 28 animals. The Orcas being one, and that the native teaching written by a Lakota Agvwa medicine person is that the first beings brought the whale along with them from the Pleiades and that **the whale is the recorder and keeper of our history and that the whale can teach us to use sound and vibration to heal**

85

us on *all levels* and that we, once, as humans, had this ability and we can tap into it again."

Art - That's very insightful. Doctor (Eaton) all over the world now, I'm hearing stories of dolphins, mostly dolphins, but whales as well, <u>healing children</u>. What can you tell us about that. The lady's right. ***They must have something we either once had or might one day have.*** I'm sure, but what is this about the <u>healings</u>? **MM** – Why not try something out of a movie to '**S.O.S.**' You remembered that in Star Trek IV, The Voyage Home it took **whales** to 'save' the earth, Art. Now James Doohan (Scottie) is suffering with Parkinson's and Alzheimer's. What if <u>we don't need</u> a *transporter* to achieve '<u>Particalization</u>,' but instead just 'beam ourselves up' Scottie.

<u>Dreamland</u> radio host, Whitley Strieber and guest, Nancy Red Star, author of *Star Ancestors,* <u>*Indian Widsomkeepers*</u> *Share the Teachings of the Extraterrestrials.* Some excerpts from that interview:

Nancy: "***<u>Thirty-eight levels</u>*** above the president are what you call ***Cosmos Clearance***. And that Clearance deals with <u>UFO's, Aliens</u> and a thing which is called <u>Particalization</u>.

Whitley: "What is that?"

Nancy: "<u>Particalization is the ability through the pineal gland</u>."

Whitley: "Pineal, the little gland in the head."

Nancy: "Yes. What that gland has the ability to do is turn ***particles into waves*** and ***waves into particles***. It's a process that can be done. There are two different forms of Reality: Particles and Waves. <u>Waves are none physical forms not limited by the confines of this or any other Universe</u>. ***The pineal gland which is located at the 3rd eye has the ability to convert waves into particles, patterns, pictures, views, configurations in accordance with*** ones holographic belief system. *We as* <u>*human beings have this unique ability*</u>. *We can create our own Tomorrow.*

MM – *T.E.W.N.C.*: **(Omni, Aug. 1989, Washington Post, Aug. 9, 1990)** On the molecular level, THC fits into receptor sites in the upper brain that seem to be <u>uniquely designed</u> to accommodate <u>THC</u>. This points to an ancient symbiosis between <u>the plant and people</u>. **MM** – *The success of the Emperor's BB 'Drugg Warr' destroyed the world's 'Natural Cannabis' food supply for our minds and bodies, while poisoning the 'Garden of Eden' with Mercury.* Seattle P.I., July 21, 2004, **"<u>Plastic left holding the bag as environmental plague. Nations around world look at a ban</u>."** by Joan Lowy. **MM** - Mattie never had access to nonpoisonous Cannabis Clothing's 'Healing Frequencies', instead he wore plastic clothes, lived in a plastic house, went to a plastic school and hospital where he was treated with *SIN*thetic petrochemical medications. Read *'The Drug Story'* by Morris A. Beale, speaking of sick *SIN*thetic buildings.

Headline News – Jan. 1, 2002 @ 6:30 am. "Some people say insurance companies don't want to write the coverage. *<u>Air quality tests</u>* at the site (*Twin Towers*) <u>show high levels of</u> <u>Mercury and Asbestos</u>. They say **it would have cost industry to much to warn about Mercury.**" **MM** – All that Mercury Vapor **escaped** from plastics, computers, concrete etc. from either being pulverized or burned in the collapse. Note: the exact same BB that engineered the W.T.C., flew the jets into the Towers and couldn't afford to warn 'ground zero' residents, rescuers and demolition crews due to the BB's dementia.

CNN Headline News, **June 23, 2004*3**, San Antonio, **Texas*4**. **It was towards the end of Fridays' show at Sea World when Ki, the killer whale, started to do his own thing.** Trainer Steve Abel *"it looked like Ki lost focus."* The Seattle Times, **June 23, 2004*3**, "9/11 Report – **We are not safe.**" **MM** – Like a movie script, **Ki** chooses this particular day **to** 'sober up' mankind, and get the children's attention.

Bill Moyers 'Trade Secrets': "There is a three hundred mile stretch along the coast where **Texas*4** and Louisiana meet that boasts the largest collection of petrochemical refineries and factories in the world. Many who live and work here call it *'Cancer Alley.'*" **MM** - Is **Ki** trying to get mankind to focus on his children's fate?

Seattle Times, July 28, 2004, **"We may be able to put and end to this suffering."** son of G.O.P. President calls for **stem cell** research. **MM** – Is Ki using Ron Reagan's Global heart felt plea to find an immediate 'cure' for Alzheimer's, Parkinson's, etc., so Mattie can announce to the world there 'is no cure' for poisoning ourselves? **Is Ki right that we are not safe from each others BB?** Time Magazine – Apr. 22, 2002, **"How Medical testing has turned Millions of Us into Guinea Pigs."**

C-Span2, July 29, 2004, **National *Immunization* Awareness Month** - National Partnership for Immunization - Julie Gerberding, M.D. of Centers for Disease Control and Prevention (CDC)…"but the vaccine we have *whether it has Thimerosal or not* is recommended for kids **because it 'saves' lives"**.

Mar./Apr. 2002, Mothering Magazine, Dr. Boyd Haley. **Thimerosal** is more toxic than Mercury and that *"giving a ten-pound infant a single vaccine in a day is the equivalent of giving a 100-pound adult 40 vaccines in a day. We are not talking about causing death; we are talking about causing Autism."* **MM** - Read *Murder by Injection* by Eustace Mullins.

Seattle Times, Dec. 15, 2003, **"Add Mercury Pollution to Bush's Dirty Deeds".** Probably the most infamous case of Mercury poisoning was in the Japanese village of Minamata. W. Eugene Smith, the great photojournalist, took the picture of the *Minamata Madonna*, gently holding her hopelessly deformed and retarded child in a steam bath, by Molly Ivins.

ALCHEMY Rediscovered and Restored by A. Cochren. Paracelsus became the first man to introduce the use of opium and *MERCURY into medicine*, and was **credited** with many miraculous cures, approximately 1608. **MM** – The BB believes in Mercury's medicinal powers. Removing **Thimerosal** would be seen as M.a.d.d.ness, throughout the spongy brained halls of **alche***demia*.

May 7, 2002, **"Dead Orca is a Red Alert."** Seattle Times, Mar. 14, 2004, **"World's Appetite for Fish Ignores Depletion of Seas."** **MM** – Now we're *all* official Skull N' Cross Bones members. USA Today, **Aug. 3, 2004*5**, **"Bush endorses idea of Intelligence** *Czarr*, '*we are a nation in danger,*' he says," by Judy Keen. Seattle Times, **Aug. 3, 2004*5**, "Eight year old Alexandra Scott, who suffered an aggressive form of pediatric *cancer* (neuroblastoma)…diagnosed just before her first birthday, started a Lemonade Stand for Cancer Research, died." Seattle P.I., Aug. 4, 2004, **"High Mercury risk in fish raises alarm"**, 'Problem a lot more widespread than we realized,' **Mercury: Emissions a key factor in fish contamination**, by Lisa Stiffler.

N.W.CableNews.com, *Aug. 6, 2004*6*, "**An Oregon <u>Mom</u> will spend almost three years in prison for blowing marijuana smoke into her kids' mouths.** Twenty-seven year old Rebecca Bass(sp) from Eugene pleaded guilty yesterday to blowing smoke into her children's **lungs** to **calm them**. Authorities say the ***CRIME*** happened almost every time the kids visited their mother in 2003. The father has custody of the 6 and 8 year old kids". **MM** – She poisoned her children with Mercury breast milk, **Thimerosal** vaccinations and they are always inhaling Mercury Vapor from their Fillings (Mercury). The **Drugg C*zarr's*** see poison as medicine. Aug. 19, 2002, "**Inside the Volatile World of the Young and Bipolar. Why are so many kids being diagnosed with the disorder once known as Manic Depression?**" ABC-WorldNewsTonight- *Aug. 6, 2004*6*, Tom Woodward's seventeen year old daughter, ***Julie, took her life*** last summer, **seven days *after she began taking the anti-depressant Zoloft.*** "<u>Our daughter would not have done this if it would not have been for the drug, and I'm convinced about that.</u>" Mothering Magazine, May/June 2004, #124, <u>Lessons from Daily Parenting</u>. "**Children are our Spiritual Teachers**". ***T.E.W.N.C.***, Chapter 7, "**Therapeutic Uses of Cannabis**", chapter 8, "**Hempseed humanity's best single food source.**"

Seattle P.I., *Aug. 6, 2004*6*, "**Colombia plan Ineffective, Drugg C*zarr* says-What's Next, Drugg C*zarr* insists that if the United States continues its efforts, supplies will run out.**" **MM** – C*zarr*s can only be *Un*-intelligent. **Luna** issued a '**red alert**' to stop our children's pain and suffering because they don't have a chance against the BB. **If some one they trust doesn't kill them**, <u>cancer will</u> or <u>their BB will convince them to commit suicide</u>. Just as Mercury destroys the brain, so do *SIN*thetic antidepressants. The **Drugg C*zarr*** will take your mother away for using a 'Natural' antidepressant medicine.

Tons of Mercury would be removed under Pentagon plan – The warehouse is a holdover from the Cold War, ***established to ensure American industry had a store of Mercury in case of warr or disaster***. see: www.ban.org/Library/assuming.pdf.

P.I., Aug. 27, 2004, "**Toxic fire retardants turn up in orcas**". Brian Kamb

E Magazine, Sept.-Oct. 2004. "**Pollution and Other Toxic Assaults Hit Women Harder Than Men. First world women face unique environmental threats. The Mercury Menace.**"

"60 Minutes' - <u>Dr. Zann</u>: "We're just **arguing** here or **discussing whether a poison is a poison**. It's a bi*zarre conversation*, you know, when you *think* about it, *to try to justify if a poison is a poison.*"

MM - If some of these dates and events have been *orca*strated, could John Lennon's song also be telling us as a group we can stop dreaming this *fr*ightmare and simply 'Imagine' 'Eden' back into reality? P.I., Sept. 6, 2004, "**Grim burials begin in Russian town.**"

Seattle Times, <u>**Sept. 11, 2004**</u>, "**Dolphin's New Buddies.**" Palestinians (children) swim with a dolphin in a private makeshift swimming pool in Gaza City yesterday. The dolphin was brought to Gaza City after being caught in a fisherman's net on the Mediterranean Sea.

USA Today, Sept. 23, 2004, "**Disturbing trend shows that terrorists see no limits on their violence.**" MM - Jesus was once a child.

Luna   Lolita is the lone survivor of a BB terrorist attack and hostage taking on Aug. 8, 1970. She has now served 34 years of imprisonment since age 6 in the Madd Hatter's Tea Cup sized 'Tank'. Quote from her video **Lolita, Slave To Entertainment**: "One doesn't have to be an expert on whales to determine that *Lolita is unhappy*. There are reports that she's on **Prozac** for her depression, but they can't be confirmed. Lolita's Medical records are no longer open to the public. They became private property, when she became property."   visit: www.slavetoentertainment.com

MM – Like something out of a movie, a dolphin materializes in Gaza City. Seven children are seen playing, hugging and holding on to 'Hope' the dolphin. Moments earlier fear dominated their world. What if **9/11/04** is remembered as the day all children were invited to join: **The We Are One Orca Human Universal Healing Frequency Projection Project**, which focuses and projects *all* of our minds 'Natural Healing Heartsongs' into the 'Great Pyramid' which mega-amplifies 'Natural Healing **Sounds**' and '**Vibrations**' into and throughout 'Mother Earth', and the solar system. **Luna** – Combining Mattie's message with Michael's allows us to *visualize the perfect holographic belief system* making it as easy as **A-B-C** and **1-2-3 to do**. #1 By *viewing* and *feeling* the musical messages contained in '**Earth Song**' and '**Heal the World**'. You see the 'Garden of Eden' re-emerging **because children and adults believe they're changing reality**. #2 Adults *must* listen to Mattie's wisdom: "The Children's Psalm…Humble yourself like a child." Why? **Luna** –Because praying can cause thinking which stops feelings due to the BB. Only the feelings of child's play automatically manifest our 'Heal the World/Heartsongs.' #3 **Luna** is calling all children: '**Will You Be There?**' at www.orcahumaninterchange.com, 'Universal Healing' **Head**quarters for **S**.imple **O**.rca **S**.olutions to all man-made problems. **By using sound and vibration to heal ourselves and the world on all levels.**

J, K and L pods thank Rebecca, Robb and Magical Ebony Woman Rabb.

p.s.:   King County Journal, Oct. 1, 2004, "**Bombings in Iraq Kill 35 children.**" Grief stricken mothers wailed on their children's bloodied corpses, as relatives collected body parts from the street. Seattle Times, Oct. 6, 2004, "**Saying Goodbye to daddy.**" P.I., Oct. 8, 2004, "A **pregnant** Israeli **woman** is wheeled into a hospital after a blast yesterday at a hotel in Taba, Egypt. **Happiness is a warm gun**, Lennon-McCartney. Oct. 9, 2004, "Just as John will never see his 64th birthday, neither will the child victims of Columbine/Kosovo/Oklahoma City/Russia's 9/11 school massacre: All victims of the BB's (***Death's Head*** – see Historychannel.com) final genocidal Wernicke's Commands. Seattle Times, Oct. 9, 2004, "**Children sketch horrors of war** – Ugandan children were forced to be soldiers or sex slaves in a brutal war." USAToday, Oct. 14, 2004, "**Pentagon resisting environmental regulation it sees as Wrongheaded.**" Let's 'Come Together' and Heal our Mercury M.A.D.D.ness now. Isn't this the Quicksilver Quickening, Art?